ALL THE GOOD GIFTS

WALLACE E. FISHER

ALL THE GOOD GIFTS

On Doing Biblical Stewardship

AUGSBURG Publishing House • Minneapolis

*To those church members who discover
in Christ the reason and the courage
to accept the cost of discipleship*

Contents

Preface

IN OUR DAY LANGUAGE HAS become flat, impoverished, and debased. Once solid, clear words now mean different things to different people. An English semanticist recently observed that in another two hundred years the American people and the English people will need an interpreter to understand one another! Language is always in danger of debasement. But since World War I, and especially after World War II, our language has been debased at an alarming rate. Because language is an extension of one's person and an evidence of God's ongoing creativity, this cultural aberration requires the church's serious attention. The problem is biblical and theological as well as cultural.

Today, more than ever, words are used not only to intimidate and coerce, but also to manipulate people and to obscure reality. Billions of dollars are spent annually on advertising geared to persuade Americans to give themselves the "best," whether they need it or not, and without any concern for the needs of others. Language has also been debased by political leaders, public school teachers, preachers, parents, teenagers, and marital partners. Inevitably, the language of Christianity has been debased, too. To Robert Schuller's followers, "doing God's will in the world" means something radically different from what it means to the disciples of Dietrich Bonhoeffer. Christian laypeople like William Stringfellow and Keith Miller, Dorothy Day and the late Kathryn Kuhlman are poles apart in their understanding and use of biblical language.

This book attempts first to rescue the word *stewardship* from inaccurate, misleading, and narrow connotations. It does so by presenting a sketch of stewardship practices in the first generation of the church (Acts-Epistles), stewardship in the church from the fourth century through the nineteenth century, and a *biblical* view of stewardship that is critical of current stewardship philosophy and practices.

Second, the book seeks to encourage and enlighten pastors and elected lay leaders who are growing in their study and practice of biblical stewardship and to challenge and motivate those who are not.

I am indebted to Abingdon Press for allowing me to draw at many points on my larger work on stewardship—*A New Climate for Stewardship*—in doing this study for church councils, sessions, vestrys, and official boards. *A New Climate* was written in 1976 as an in-depth resource book for study groups in congregations, new members' classes, lecture-discussion sessions in the adult church school, and extended sermon series. I hope church councils, using this little book, will authorize the use of the more detailed study in their congregations. Further, where I have written previously in some depth on matters that are only touched lightly in this work, I have cited those books in the notes.

I also thank my colleagues in the American Lutheran Church, especially Mr. John Dewey, Division for Life and Mission in the Congregation, for providing the reason for doing this introductory study on biblical stewardship. And I am especially grateful to the laypeople and my fellow-clergy (past and present) in the Lutheran Church of the Holy Trinity, Lancaster, Pennsylvania, who, over the last quarter of a century, have struggled doggedly and painfully, spontaneously and joyfully to learn and begin to do biblical stewardship. This book, like my larger study on stewardship, reflects this aspect of our life together. Because of their response, what I write here is tried and proven. Slowly, the Protestant church in the United States is coming to the realization that biblical preaching, evangelical teaching, sacraments, and relevant theology define its mission in the world today.

WALLACE E. FISHER

1

HOW
THE CHURCH
HAS RECEIVED MONEY

BIBLICAL STEWARDSHIP INVOLVES MORE than motivating church members to give money and property and stocks and bonds to the church for Christ's work, although that is part of it. Actually, the word *stewardship* has come into wide usage in the church only in the twentieth century, especially since World War II. This recent usage tied stewardship narrowly to the congregation's annual budget, every member visitation (or other means for receiving pledges), signed pledges, apportionments and other benevolence objectives, and the financing of the local church. In most churches, therefore, stewardship, like evangelism, is a program carried out under the supervision of a council committee comprised of people who "like that sort of thing" or those who do it like galley slaves to keep the local congregation in existence.

Glowing exceptions to this appraisal of stewardship and evangelism in American Protestantism only serve to highlight its accuracy.

We shall be helped in getting at the biblical view of stewardship if we recall briefly how, over the centuries, the church has addressed itself to the material aspects of its existence. The Pauline Epistles and the Book of Acts are our primary sources for discovering how the early church received and used money. There we discover that money was asked for unapologetically by the apostles and missionaries and given for the support of the apostles, missionaries, and evangelists so that they could engage full time in Christ's ministry; for the relief of the sick and the poor in the local assembly of believers and their hard-pressed fellow-believers in other small congregations around the Mediterranean; and for the general expenses of public worship in the local congregations.

During the early decades of the Christian church when its constituency was economically poor and sporadically persecuted, giving was Christ-centered. It was motivated by gratitude to God for his amazing grace in Jesus, his reconciling and liberating work in Christ. But even in those pristine years motivation was not everywhere pure or giving altogether spontaneous: the "stingy" Christians at Corinth; Demas, who, having "loved this present world," forsook the missionary trail with Paul to return to Thessalonica to live there a decent but self-indulgent life; and that avaricious, devious couple, Ananias and Sapphira. Present-day Christians must guard against idealizing the redeemed yet still marred human creatures who made up the early church. A cursory reading of Paul's two letters to the church at Corinth provides a realistic perspective on early Christian belief and behavior! Nonetheless, we who live in congregations where the Spirit of Christ is alive but not dominant—and in some cases barely evident—need to remember gratefully that the diverse band of men and women who constituted the early church were the stalwarts-in-Christ of whom T. R. Glover wrote early in the twentieth century: they "out-loved, out-gave, and out-died" the devotees of the other religions and cults.

The core membership of the early church, committed to Christ and motivated by gratitude to God, shaped their life-style to reflect Christ's mind. Hundreds of Christians were exiled or executed during the intermittent persecutions in the first three centuries because they would not renounce their allegiance to Christ. The blood of the martyrs nurtured the early church. Fidelity to God's Word then and now is the supreme test of biblical stewardship. There are some evidences of this stewardship in our era but they are scattered: Bonhoeffer, King, Evers, Reeb, Stringfellow, the Berrigans, and a handful of clergy and laity in congregations from Maine to California, South Africa to Hungary, South Korea to Brazil. This remnant seeks to place God first in daily living.

When Christianity became not only a legal religion but the preferred religion of the decadent Roman Empire in the early fourth century, the church received members en masse. The level of corporate commitment dropped notably. This reality, together with the steady institutionalization of the church after the fourth century, affected adversely the biblical stewardship practiced by the early Christians. Motivation for giving changed from gratitude for God's grace to an institutionally bred compulsion to earn God's approval. Late in the fourth century, salvation by merit had become the primary motivating factor for giving to the ecclesiastical establishment, as it had been the Pharisees' basic motivation for giving in Jesus' day. Clement of Alexandria advised Christians that "alms lighten the burden of sin." Chrysostom set the foundation for Tetzel's extravagant claims in selling indulgences in the sixteenth century, preaching that "there is no sin which alms cannot cleanse." In spite of protests here and there, both the concept and practice of salvation by merit grew steadily until, during the decadent papacy of Leo X, Luther attacked it frontally. What began as an attack on "giving" to the church to buy salvation ended in the formal recovery of the evangelical principle for a substantial segment of Western Christendom. In 1517, Tetzel's anvil (salvation by meritorious deeds) provided the striking base for Luther's hammer (salvation by grace).

Unfortunately, Luther, who initially advocated voluntary giving, accepted not only the protection of German princes for the evangelical churches but also endorsed their right to gather proscribed church tithes and taxes. This "required" giving was characteristic of the Protestant state churches in Europe after the Reformation. It was one reason among others why West Europeans risked settlement in the wilderness of North America.

But old ways die hard. By 1650, the established church in New England was state-supported. Dissenters, free-thinkers, Quakers, and Baptists were well advised to settle on the "frontier" (now Rhode Island) or flee to Pennsylvania which neither made legal demands for religious conformity nor required "church taxes." When the English took over the Dutch New Netherlands in the 1660s, the crown taxed *all* the citizens to support the Anglican Church. Shortly after settlements were made in Virginia and the Carolinas, tithes (church taxes) were collected in the form of tobacco and other commodities by royal governors to support the Anglican Church in those royal, English colonies. The Virginia Assembly enacted the *first* church support law in the New World in 1621. But as West Europeans had become restless under a forced support of an established church in the seventeenth century, bitter discontent with the practice emerged early in the New World. The famous "Parson's Case" became a strand in the doctrine of church-state separation in America when the Virginia clergy sued their fellow colonials in the court for the full tithe due on tobacco, a legal obligation not paid in full because of a drought. The English king and the royal governor were allied against the colonists; both supported the suit brought by the Anglican clergy of Virginia. A frontier lawyer who would gain wide recognition as a fomenter of the American Revolution, Patrick Henry, took the case in behalf of the people and won it. A few decades later the issue would be one of the causes for rebellion. The Federal Constitution, framed in 1787 and amended radically by the several states, guaranteed freedom of religion. By 1830, the last state law authorizing a tax for an established church was expunged by the Massachusetts legislature.

But from the beginning, the colonial churches also asked for and received additional monies for church support through pew rents, subscription lists, lotteries, and voluntary offerings. Pew rents existed in the church I serve from 1730 until 1946, when my predecessor, with the support of the vestry, abolished them.[1] Trinity Church paid for its magnificent tower and steeple, built, 1785-1794, with monies received from a lottery authorized, on petition from Trinity's vestry, by the Pennsylvania State Legislature! Free-will offerings became the way of church support only slowly in nineteenth century America. During the early twentieth century, carefully-drawn budgets shared with the congregation, every-member visitations, signed pledge cards, and envelopes became a firm strand in mainline Protestant church life.

Luther P. Powell, in Kenneth Thompson's *Stewardship in Contemporary Theology*, observes that money can be transferred "by theft, by chance, by exchange, and by gift." The American church has employed all four of these means: lotteries and other games of chance, merchandising, and free-will offerings. In the late nineteenth century, Washington Gladden charged—and a number of Christians and non-Christians took up that charge again in the 1960s—that the church also used "stolen monies" for its support. Gladden pointed to John D. Rockefeller as a prime example. Present-day critics point to sources from which the church receives monies that could not possibly be "laundered." This is a complex issue with no easy solution. But the church needs to admit the validity of the charge, and its lay leaders and clergy need to effect those changes which the gospel persuades them to make.

Looking back across the centuries, we learn that the church has used many different methods for getting people to contribute money for its institutional life. We also learn that when the institutional church achieves a measure of strength and power, both clergy and laity tend to lose sight of the biblical truth that the church's ministry exists to serve persons rather than to enhance its own institutional life. The church in the fifteenth century, just before the Reformation, reached the high-water mark of institutionalism. But the practice persists. Both Protestant and Roman Catholic churches hedged their bets carefully in the Nazi state, 1937-1942. Both were protective of their institutional life in America during the Vietnam War, especially before the Tet offensive in 1968. Scarcely a handful of Christians in Europe or the Americas have taken seriously Dietrich Bonhoeffer's dictum, "When Christ calls a man, he bids him come and die." The old Adam in Bonhoeffer died a thousand times before he was hanged in Flossenberg Prison, 9 April, 1945! That is the continuing cost of Christian discipleship. Of course, Bonhoeffer was echoing Jesus who said plainly that his disciples are those who take up their cross daily, discipline themselves, and follow him.

Another lesson we learn from church history is

that pressing financial needs of the institutional church (congregational, district, national, global) tempt clergy and lay leaders to exploit the human motives of fear, pride, and greed in raising monies for the church. Today, too, manipulative methods for "raising" money are used in varying degrees by the church. Present-day measures employed by professional fund raisers collide head-on with biblical stewardship. Examined honestly, it is evident that they violate evangelical freedom and demean persons by viewing them as objects to be manipulated. In many congregations, these unevangelical practices are employed in raising the annual budget.

Since the church is institutionally-framed as well as God-ordained and people-oriented, this broad survey of the methods the church has used to get money over the centuries (and in many quarters still does), provides perspective on what we want to say about stewardship in this booklet. We also need to get another perspective if we want to understand and do biblical stewardship in our culture: the rise of "impersonal" giving in an industrialized-technocratic society. Consequently, we shall examine American society.

At the time of the American Revolution, there were only a handful of Christians in the thirteen colonies. The statistics—inaccurate, yet broadly indicative—reveal that only one person in twenty-five was an active member of any church. What we call "benevolence" was done neighbor to neighbor in colonial days. When the Methodist church began to follow the American frontier, especially after 1800, its members were asked to support what some churches still call "home missions" as well as special missions to the American Indians. In the nineteenth century the church in West Europe and America focused its "missionary" attention on Asia and Africa. The great missionary movement became the dominant characteristic of the church in the West in the last century.[2] Since the majority of church members were neither able nor inclined to go to India or Liberia, China or Japan to do "missionary work," missionaries were called, appointed, and supported by congregations in concert and/or by missionary societies in the several congregations. Individual contributions of material goods were gathered into a general treasury for missionary work. Person-to-person benevolence was not possible when the church followed the American frontier and began to support "foreign missions." Today, this impersonal character of giving prevails at virtually all levels of the church's benevolence work. It is also characteristic of our present public philanthropy and community-based responses to human need in local communities.

These new ways of doing good to one's neighbor reflect two radical social-economic changes in American society and in its relationship with other nations. The first occurred in the period from 1890-1930: the closing of the American frontier, the emergence of a predominant urban industrial society, the quest for social justice (1900-1914), the rise of economic imperialism (1900-1978), and "the war to make the world safe for democracy" (1914-1918). The second period was from 1930-1978: The Great Depression, public welfare, social security, World War II, the Cold War, the Fair Deal, the New Frontier, the Great Society, Watergate, the energy crisis, world hunger, worldwide inflation.

A money economy, which developed steadily after the fourteenth century in Europe, came to dominate life in America with the rise of an urban-industrial society after the Civil War. In the twentieth century, this money economy has spread over the world, especially since 1950. Modern men and women work for money in various forms; it is, along with credit, the common medium of our economic exchange. How one gets his or her money as well as how one spends it is, therefore, an expression and extension of one's person. Philip Guadella, the gifted biographer of the Duke of Wellington, declared at the close of his painstaking research that if he had Wellington's cancelled checks he would know what kind of man the Duke was! The cancelled checks of ordained and lay members of our Christian congregations in America would not tell us everything about the quality of their faith and life, but it would reveal solidly their priorities in life.

In our crassly materialistic culture, the getting and using of money, goods, and property demands our primary energies. Wordsworth, distressed about the impact of an industrialized English society in the nineteenth century, observed, "Getting and spending, we lay waste our powers." What would he say in our affluent society? Certainly, *how* we get our material holdings and *how* we use our economic resources are massive tests of our personal commitment to Christ in a materialistic culture.[3] This impersonal, complex, ambiguous style of getting and spending money needs to be faced head-on and discussed openly in the light of the gospel in every congregation.

During my three decades of parish ministry, I have not met a single church member, ordained or lay, who, like the widow who gave her mite, gave his or her last dollar for the work of Christ. Nor have I met a member of the church, ordained or lay, who, like Zacchaeus on coming to himself in the hour that Christ recognized and penetrated his awful loneliness and isolation, gave a half of his goods to charitable works and paid fourfold reparations to those whom he had wronged. But I have been privileged to know hundreds of people in a particular parish who, taking Jesus Christ seriously and seeking to exercise a responsible stewardship of their person and possessions, have moved from giving less than one percent to five and ten and fifteen percent, and, in one case I know, thirty percent of their incomes for church and community services. That has happened—and continues to happen—because we set out to learn and do biblical stewardship. We are still learning.

What then, is biblical stewardship? That is the theme of the next chapter.

For Discussion

1. How does our congregation receive money to meet its annual budget?

2. If an every-member visitation is employed, is it effective? By what criteria?

3. The church has been persecuted in many places over the centuries, beginning with the first Christian century. Where is the church being persecuted today? In what ways? For what reasons? Is the Christian church persecuted in the United States? Discuss.

4. Does the church grow stronger in seasons of persecution? Does persecution weaken the church? Can persecution destroy the church? Discuss.

5. Does our congregation or denomination use "stolen" money? Does the Protestant church in America use "stolen" money? What, according to the thinking in our church, is "benevolence"?

6. Ramsay Clark, controversial attorney general in Lyndon Johnson's administration and advocate for poor and oppressed persons, said recently, "I do believe that materialism is the great failing of the American people. Our whole value patterns are based on greed. We measure success in terms of accumulation of wealth." Does Clark's observation apply to (a) our congregation, (b) our community, (c) our national church, (d) our state government, (e) our national government? Be specific.

7. The biblical story of Zacchaeus is well known in the church. This "born again" businessman decided to pay reparations to those whom he had abused economically. Should Christians pay reparations to the one-third of our fellow-citizens who are ill-fed, ill-housed, and discriminated against; and to persons in the third and fourth worlds? Is great-hearted stewardship a mark of "born again" Christians?

2

WHAT IS
BIBLICAL
STEWARDSHIP?

T HE CHURCH MUST CLEAR AWAY its alliterative, narrow, compartmentalized, ecclesiastical description of stewardship—"time, talent, and treasure"—if it wants to do biblical stewardship. In most congregations this worn-out phrase means giving a little money, a modicum of time, and modest talent for the work of the local congregation, district, and national church. Few congregations challenge their members to serve actively in the secular community and to give generously to meet the needs of their hard-pressed neighbors. Some congregations are retreats and/or parasites in their community setting. Few congregations encourage and equip their members to speak out as informed citizens or endeavor to persuade them to be active in government at the local, state, and national levels. In any society, but especially in a democratic society, responsible citizenship is part of biblical stewardship (cf. Chapter 5).

Another area to be examined honestly before most congregations can get deeply into biblical stewardship, let alone practice it, is the current parochialism that characterizes most Protestant congregations. Because white, middle-class and upper-class Americans are the backbone of mainline Protestant churches and because the majority of the clergy are "recruited" from this class, the problem is indigenous in the life of mainline Protestantism. This branch of American Christianity exhibits the cultural strengths and weaknesses of the middle-class. At the grass roots, scarcely a segment of its constituency has been converted to the gospel's world-view and concern for *all* people. This means that many of these congregations are in fact conservative, subtly racist, class conscious, and, in some places, preoccupied with institutional survival.

A third area to be addressed in getting at biblical stewardship is the American's materialistic view of life. We live daily in terms of the things we handle, touch, taste, see, and smell. In our affluent society, these are legion. Locked to the present moment, we forget our roots in the past and entertain no enlivening hope for our future.

Eschatology, a dominant strand in Jesus' teaching, is scarcely a thin strand in mainline Protestant preaching today. Decent church members decide, often unconsciously because of their culturally created views of consumerism and obsolescence, to honor convenience above conscience and to seek comfort rather than character. They have little or no sense of transcendent judgment or of lively hope.

Keeping alert to these ecclesiastical and cultural forces, we turn our attention now to a working view of biblical stewardship. A solid place to begin our inquiry is with a broad description of Jesus' life-style and teachings. He is, after all, the Christian's proper model.

Jesus valued all life in this world; and he was grateful for his own life. He declared repeatedly that his life—and all life—was given by God. He enjoyed his Father's creation. Jesus was not a monastic. Except for his two or three years of public ministry, he worked at a trade to support himself and his mother. He was neither a mendicant nor a mystic. His appreciation of good food and wine prompted his enemies to call him a wine-bibber and a glutton. Jesus was not an ascetic. Enjoying the whole of life, he wanted everyone to share not only in the life of the spirit but also to enjoy the fruits of the earth. He urged the Rich Young Ruler to sell everything he had, not because earthly goods are intrinsically bad, but because the Rich Young Ruler valued his possessions more highly than he should. When Zacchaeus adopted a life-style oriented to persons rather than to property, Jesus commended him. He did not direct him to give away all that was left. The Good Samaritan was, Jesus said, the only responsible steward on the Jericho road the day bandits mugged a traveler. The religious professionals who traveled that road that same day failed God because they had failed to help a human being in need. If one's experience on the Damascus Road is authentic, he or she serves persons in need on the Jericho Roads of daily living.

Jesus, according to the gospel accounts, spoke five times more frequently about earthly possessions than about prayer. His person embodied his message, touching real people in a real world. Many American church people, on hearing Jesus speak about hunger, money, justice, and honesty would complain: "He's not spiritual." This contemporary overspiritualization of Jesus' person and message denies not only God's creation but also God himself. The church in many quarters is more "spiritual" (other-worldly) than God who is infinitely close to his creation, and loves it deeply.

Jesus encouraged his followers to seek first the kingdom of God. He did not call them to poverty, celibacy, fasting, or prayer as ends in themselves. Some followers were poor, others fasted, and a few elected celibacy. Many gave themselves to long seasons of intercessory prayer. But in the case of each, it was a matter of personal choice or personal situation. Jesus did not define any of those practices except prayer as requirements for discipleship. Every petition in the prayer that he taught his disciples, while set in an eschatological frame of reference, relates concretely to life here and now. His concern for diseased and broken bodies was as intense as his concern for disturbed minds and depressed spirits. Jesus viewed the kingdom of God in its fullness as a coming event; he also rejoiced in it as a present reality. Salvation for him was a present experience as well as a future hope; it was mundane *and* eschatological. Eternal life begins here and now through commitment to Christ. So, we work for the kingdom even as we wait for its full coming.[4]

The truth of the biblical ethic is proved in human history. It focuses on every facet of human existence in the broad context of God's creation. Neither Jesus' teaching nor his life-style suggests or implies that the material is evil and the spiritual good. He fulfilled and enlarged the Old Testament teaching that God's Spirit lays claim to the whole person. Biblical Christianity is not dualistic; spirit and body are one in the whole person under God. From Genesis to Revelation, the biblical view is consistent: God's Spirit claims the human body, mind, and spirit. God works in, not outside history.

Present-day church members need to study Genesis and Deuteronomy, the Psalms and Job, Hosea and Jeremiah before they can appreciate

Jesus fully. Biblical revelation, like biblical ethics, is of the earth, earthy. Twenty-five centuries before our Founding Fathers wrote, "We, the people of the United States, in order to form a more perfect union, *establish justice* . . . ," Amos and Micah had called for social justice in God's behalf. Alexander Hamilton echoed the Hebrew prophets when he averred: "I think the first duty of society is justice." As the ghost of Marley plagued Scrooge, so the spirit of Marcion (spiritualization of Jesus and his gospel) haunts contemporary church members who never heard of Marcion! The contemporary church neglects the Old Testament—a substantial part of God's self-revelation; it fails to appreciate Jesus' heritage; and it divorces him from *our* history. To understand God's deed-in-Christ we must appreciate the historical context in which God acted to liberate humanity, and continues to act in the resurrected Christ. God's stewardship calls us to be responsible custodians of his goodness in the context of *our* history, here and now.[5]

God, having created the universe and all life, looked on his creation and declared it to be good. He took pleasure in it. When human beings, his crowning labor of love fashioned in his own image, turned their backs on him, he did not wash his hands of them, bribe them to come home, cajole them into accepting him, or coerce them into obedience. He set out instead in their own experience to reconcile the rebels for his own sake as well as theirs. God revealed his purpose and person, not in the whirlwind and the fire, but in the grandeur and misery of human experience where he would be understood. From the distant days of Abraham to the tense political era of John the Baptist, the Hebrews had caught glimpses of God acting in history. Then, in his own time, God entered into the human experience himself, born of a woman, bone of our bone and flesh of our flesh, subject to family disciplines, accepting finally the temporal domination of the state. The Incarnation also demonstrates what human beings can become when God's Spirit frees them, inhabits them, gives his mind to them. God does not view humans as disembodied spirits. He is interested in more than "religion," or as it is put these days, "spirituality." William Temple was fond of declaring that Christianity is the most materialistic of the world religions. And so it is! It is of the good earth, earthy.

Appropriately, the English origin of the word *stewardship* is earthy. The steward was the keeper of an enclosure for livestock, the caretaker (ward) of another's property (sty). This Anglo-Saxon word was the counterpart of the Greek word, *oikonomos*, which means, literally, the manager of a house. Both meanings incorporate these concepts: an entrustment by the owner; a responsible servant; a final accounting.

Jesus viewed the steward as the willing custodian of what God has entrusted to his people for a season: human, animal, and plant life, the earth and seas, and especially his gospel. He taught that God holds each steward accountable for the management of what is committed to him. He also demonstrated his radical teaching. The concept of stewardship in the Old Testament calls for responsible trusteeship. Jesus accepted that concept only to enlarge it. Jesus called for personal *initiative*, active risk-taking in one's stewardship (parable of the talents).

Paul's understanding of stewardship incorporates the main strands of Jesus' teaching. Essentially, the Apostle saw himself as a steward of the mysteries of God—the Word itself. He also described God's total plan of salvation as *God's* stewardship. His argument, forged in an inimical society and a humanly defective church, is on this order. God's stewardship is his personal plan for the redemption of the world through his Son's birth as a human being, his life, teachings, death, resurrection, and victorious presence in the world. God incarnate, the risen Christ, enables his co-laborers in his church to reclaim God's lost world. Paul argues that this divine-human fellowship is unique because it is the only community on earth that has been entrusted with the true mysteries of God. The head of this fellowship is Christ, God's Chief Steward, who does his

Father's will and enables his followers to be his co-stewards. The four evangelists testify to Jesus' *absolute* obedience to God's will. The *essence* of Christian stewardship, then, is to do God's will with Christ as guide and support. This stewardship is every Christian's true vocation. The community of persons called and empowered to take up this task is Christ's church. The gospel, the church, and God's stewardship are inextricably bound together. To separate any one from the other two is to obscure God's self-revelation and distort the purpose of Christ's church.[6] Biblical stewardship is not a fund raising process that keeps the church "running." It is every Christian's essential vocation. The church is responsible to God for its proper custodianship of his good gifts—life, earth, cosmos, and his Word.

Jesus' stewardship of God's mysteries is the living model for his followers. He allowed nothing to deter him from going where God asked him to go and doing what God wanted him to do. When Peter tried to dissuade his dearest friend from going to Jerusalem—God's clear course for his Son—Jesus reminded him of his central mission: "The Son of man came not to be served but to serve, and to give his life as a ransom for many" (Mark 10:45). Jesus committed himself to God's plan of salvation; that was his stewardship. It is the church's only stewardship if it wants to be true to Christ.

In the New Testament then, these basic meanings of stewardship can be identified:

(1) the steward is an overseer, a caretaker, a household manager—not an owner—who is expected to take the initiative in managing God's gifts (Jesus' parables)

(2) the steward is entrusted with the gospel by God himself (Paul's Epistles)

(3) this stewardship is every Christian's task in God's plan of salvation (Prison Epistles).[7]

This elementary summary, studied in depth by pastor and lay leaders, is kept before the whole congregation through biblical preaching, evangelical teaching, the sacraments, pastoral care, and personal and corporate witness in the world. We shall expand this broad view of biblical stewardship and consider some of its theological and practical implications in Chapter 3.

For Discussion

1. Do you think the alliterative phrase, "time, talent, and treasure," is meaningful to people in our congregation? Is it meaningful to you? Why? Why not?

2. Is our congregation economically stable? Do we have affluent members? What constitutes affluence in our community? Is our congregation a mixture of social and economic classes and several or more races? Why? Why not? Does our congregation relate to and attract the oppressed and the depressed? Why? Why not?

3. Does our congregation—in its preaching, teaching, and giving—reflect a parochial view of life or a community view? A national view or a global view?

4. Is it possible to accept Jesus Christ as personal Savior, worship him weekly, and pray to him daily, yet show little concern for people who differ from our congregation's constituency in color, creed, race, and/or economic background at home and abroad? Discuss.

5. One need not be a theologian to recognize that any person can be a church member today without loving or obeying Jesus Christ. But is it possible, as some earnest people contend, to believe in Jesus Christ, love him, and serve him without being a member of a particular congregation? Document your arguments biblically and theologically.

6. What is your personal understanding of the relationship between the Word of God and the Spirit-prompted human words which constitute the Bible? What does our denomination teach on this crucial issue? What is the relationship between revelation and history? Can revelation be viewed *as* history? Discuss.

7. In what ways does God make himself known to men and women today? How do you know? What did Luther mean, "My conscience is captive to the Word of God?"

8. Discuss the relationship between biblical stewardship and God's plan of salvation. Is biblical stewardship corporate, personal, or both? Discuss. In this chapter we identified three distinguishing marks of the biblical steward. How do they apply in our congregation?

3

SOME
IMPLICATIONS OF
BIBLICAL STEWARDSHIP

A GAINST THE BROAD OVERVIEW of biblical stewardship presented in the last chapter, we shall focus now on some of its theological and practical implications in our time and place.

First and foremost, there is the church's stewardship of biblical truth, God's Word. This is the church's primary service to God and the world. How the church discerns the Word of God couched in the Spirit-prompted words of human beings, how it teaches the relationship between the Word and the Bible, how it understands revelation *in* history and *as* history, and how it applies biblical truth in concrete situations determine whether its custodianship (stewardship) of God's Word is responsible or not.

Mainline Protestant churches agree substantially

that the Word of God is the Good News of God's saving work in Christ. They accept it as the message about the essential nature and purpose of God's saving activity initiated at creation and revealed progressively through myth, legend, drama, poetry, apocalyptic literature, historical events, persons such as Amos, Hosea, and John the Baptist, and pre-eminently in the person of Jesus of Nazareth. All Protestants agree that scripture is the Word of God —the Spirit-prompted record of *human* witness to God's saving activity in history. Mainline Protestant denominations also agree that the key to interpreting all scripture is the person, teaching, and work of Jesus Christ. That was Luther's view: "If the scriptures themselves, as a whole, claim to be the Word of God, they can be this only if they are, as a whole, interpreted in terms of Christ. . . . Christ is Lord of the scriptures." The biblical account of God's saving activity is more than a report. The Christ-event, rooted in an identifiable moment of history (Barth), is not bound by history (Bultmann). Revelation provides a new view of history (Pannenberg).

Biblical scholarship exists to help the church preach and teach the whole counsel of God. If the church is to do this effectively, biblical scholarship must find a place in each congregation's teaching ministry. The pulpit (catechetical sermons), church school classes (content and methodology),

and small study groups (dialog and application)
are employed so that laypeople are equipped to discern God's Word in the Spirit-prompted language
of those (known and anonymous) who wrote the
biblical texts. Genuine biblical scholarship is not
bound by the traditions of church or sect. It seeks
to discern the divine Word in the biblical record.
This significant aspect of stewardship must be cul-
tivated and exercised in every congregation. Each
congregation should be a "seminary" for lay people.
This is part of its proper stewardship of God's
Word. The magisterial office, the Reformation reminds us, is a primary function of ministry. The
clergy must recover it, exercise it, and teach the
laity to exercise it. To be sure, biblical scholarship
is a means, not an end. It does not constitute a new
"authority" that stands above God's authority as it
is revealed in scripture. Some Protestants, properly
alert to the obscurantism and intolerance bred by
those who make the Bible a "paper pope," become
obscurantists and disdainers themselves by making
historical criticism and/or *their doctrine* of the
Word idols that are honored above Christ himself.
Christ is Lord of the church. He is the Lord of the
earth. He is also the Lord of the scriptures.

One evidence that a congregation is a responsible
custodian of God's Word is its willingness to accept
this teaching responsibility and to act on it.[8] The
pastor is the chief teacher; but he or she is not the

only teacher. The elected lay leaders' primary responsibility is biblical and theological before it is administrative. Trained clergy, the Reformers averred, are appointed to teach laypeople God's truth, serve them from its resources, and reflect on and act in the light of his revelation. The lay leaders are responsible for seeing that the Word of God is rightly preached and taught by the full-time ministers *and* the part-time ministers, the appointed lay teachers; that the sacraments are properly administered; that the whole congregation learns and teaches God's Word and acts on it in the world. Christian worship in the sanctuary and service to others in the world are inseparable; together they constitute our proper stewardship of God's gifts. Until the two are joined in local congregations, Jesus will be imprisoned in a book or obscured by the mists of value judgments—the God nobody knows. A critical, faithful custodianship of the Word also guards against the limitations inherent in demythologization and symbolism. It exposes literalism and moralism. Further, it provides a solid perspective for evaluating and appreciating "charismatic gifts" in the congregation. This critical custodianship of God's Word—and the intelligible proclamation and teaching of it—is the church's primary stewardship.

Scripture testifies that the primary objective of all Christian ministry is to bring salvation to the human spirit, or, in the idiom of the day, "liberation" to all imprisoned spirits. This objective calls for the forthright proclamation of the good news that God acted decisively in Jesus to liberate all people from sin, demonic forces, and death. The church—the body of Christ, the new humanity, the people of God—is the community in which one meets this saving God in preaching and teaching and sacraments and caring and service in the world.

Second, a proper stewardship of the Word calls the church to safeguard apostolic truth. It is the historic task of the church not only to proclaim and teach apostolic truth but also to be its apologist (defender) against all enemies within or outside its community. Paul emphasized this strongly. More than a decade ago, Friedrich Gogarten warned that the most serious threats to the gospel today, against which it must be guarded, are its being dissolved into a myth or hardened into a religion of law. Many Protestants understand that in principle. Most, however, find it hard to act on that principle. There *is* moralistic preaching and teaching in some quarters of mainline Protestantism. There *is* the preaching of cheap grace in other quarters of the church. This is poor stewardship. God will hold us accountable.

There are other dangers against which the church must guard apostolic truth these days. Many congregations present the Word of God in preaching and teaching forms and styles that make it appear to be irrelevant. In some places the hand of a dead orthodoxy obscures the vibrant, powerful, gracious Word of God. On the other hand, some congregations are so eager to be relevant that they trim down the *fundamentals* of the faith, denying in effect the theology of the cross. Safeguarding apostolic truth is a firm strand in biblical stewardship.

Third, the church's custodianship of the gospel calls it to *do* God's truth. The church exists to obey Christ's commands in the world. It is fashioned to act out God's purposes in human society. This calls for priestly service to all people without regard for their condition, color, or creed. It calls for a person-to-person witness that is intelligible to secular people in *their* cultural milieu. It also requires each congregation to bring persons, ideas, social mores, and social, political, and economic institutions under the judgment of God's Word. If the church were in fact doing God's truth valiantly in his strength today there would be sharper tensions and deeper conflicts between secular society and the church. Biblical stewardship requires us to please God rather than people.[9] Too often in the contemporary church, it is the other way around.

But getting the gospel into the world requires not only a disciplined and dedicated Christian personnel; it also requires money. Whether the local congregation employs a unified budget, pledge

cards, and envelopes or relies on love gifts the issue is the same: until the local congregation uses
"unrighteous mammon" to make friends for the
kingdom it is not the whole body of Christ. Scripture provides evidence that the church, from the
beginning, was concerned to provide material gifts
for widows and orphans and, through additional
gifts, to proclaim the gospel to the Gentile world.
To fuss and fume, to argue meanly over "benevolence," or to drag one's feet as some church councils and congregations do, fractures the biblical
image of stewardship. That needs to be faced honestly in parish after parish in this day and age.

But benevolence cannot be divided as neatly as
most mainline Protestant churches have supposed:
3 to 1, 2 to 1, or 50-50. A congregation's *outreach*
will never equal human needs. There is no ceiling
in a world like ours. But biblical giving is also
inreach and community-oriented. A parish that
does not provide economic support (help with
rents and fuel, groceries, psychiatric services for
those in need) *in* its own fellowship, scholarship
aid for its own promising young people, and *community service* is *not* a benevolent church no matter how regularly it meets a mechanically devised
apportionment.

Here are two questions which, answered honestly, reveal a congregation's basic commitment to
biblical stewardship:

(1) Does our congregation recognize gladly and humbly that it was bought for a price, the precious blood of its Lord and Savior, Jesus Christ? Granted, one can turn this question into a shibboleth or sentimental drivel. But where a community of people gathered in the name of God remembers gladly that it was bought for a price, the precious blood of Jesus Christ, and thinks on that and feels deeply about it and acts on it, biblical stewardship is generated.

(2) Does our congregation recognize that, having been bought for a price, it was bought for a *purpose* — the doing of Christ's ministry in the world beginning in its own community and reaching to the outermost parts of the earth? When a congregation truly remembers in its worship and its teaching, its preaching and its administering of its life that it was *bought* to *do* Christ's ministry here and now, and acts on that remembrance, biblical stewardship results.

The church is true to the stewardship of "the mysteries of God" (gospel) when, at the grass roots, it proclaims and teaches God's mysteries revealed in Christ and from those resources motivates its constituency to let Christ inhabit their persons and through them to serve others in the world. This custodianship of the Word and care of persons is every congregation's first act of biblical stewardship.

Certainly the first step in caring for persons in the congregation and for nonmembers through the congregation is to persuade and enable the former to discern, accept, and incarnate the living Word of God in their persons so that they can persuade the latter to take an active place in Christ's church; and to encourage both to work for a just society for the sake of God and humanity. Personal evangelism and social action are inseparable strands in the responsible congregation's proper stewardship of God's Word. I have dealt with this aspect of stewardship more fully in my book on evangelism.[10] Here, we identify it as an area for practical consideration in fashioning a useful theology of Christian stewardship.

Another focus for fashioning a theology of stewardship is a biblical stewardship of the self. John Wesley prayed: "O Lord, let us not live to be useless." Modern medicine and medical technology have added years to our lives. Dudley White, the heart specialist who attended Dwight Eisenhower more than twenty years ago, said then: "We need to get more life into our years." Christian stewardship of the self is a direct road to doing that. But first the church must fill its own members with the call to be good stewards of the self.

First, consider time and the self. The gospel

equips us to handle the past with its successes over which we tend to boast and its failures over which we tend to brood. It enables us to use the present constructively by requiring orderliness, spontaneity, and self-discipline in the context of freedom. The gospel also enables us to cope creatively with a future which frightens and intimidates us when we face it alone.

Second, the gospel instructs us in the proper use of human resources. Paul speaks about the variety of gifts. No person possesses all gifts. Each, however gifted, needs the contributions and support of others to live fully. A secular demonstration of this truth comes readily to mind. People who live in white suburbia are no less ghettoed and culturally impoverished than people who live in Appalachia or urban slums. Too often church people cut themselves off from the riches in other cultures by living only with their own kind. Our nation is beginning to recognize that it cannot force its will on others in the world, that it has much to learn from others, that it is inter-dependent. The third world is coming into its own and the fourth world is crying out to be helped. Talk about interdependence and a "global village" is no longer rhetoric. It is reality.

But focusing exclusively on a person's particular talent(s) rather than on the whole person denigrates the individual. It is necessary, to be sure, to

take one's talent(s) into consideration for responsible tasks in any social institution. It is hurtful to
the person, however, and disruptive to the community if the primary focus is fixed firmly on the
talent or skill rather than on the person. Church
leaders at all levels work diligently to enlist church
members to serve the institutional church. They
lag badly in motivating them to serve God in a
broken world. Unless the congregation is a fellowship in which its members learn to serve others in
the world for Christ's sake, it is not a responsible
steward of the mysteries of God. When Jesus' disciples came to him with their discovery that people other than they were doing good works, Jesus
advised them that God's work was also being ac-
complished in different ways, in different places,
through persons other than themselves. Clergy and
laity alike tend to limit God's liberating work to
their parochial understanding of and participation
in it. That is natural; but it is not Christian.

Biblical stewardship also looks to God's Spirit to
transform one's personal disadvantages into advan-
tages for effective Christian ministry. Biblical
stewardship reminds us that God uses flawed people to do his work. *No one else is available.* We are
all flawed. One's human resources include the whole
of one's experience. Some church people fail to use
their victories as well as their defeats as learning
experiences in the hard journey toward responsible

personhood. Christian stewardship sees all human "successes" as God's grace in action. As Paul said to the church at Corinth: "Don't be so proud. What do you have that was not given to you by God?"

Biblical stewardship teaches persons how to cope with failure. Personal failure is a continuing strand in human experience. A proper stewardship of the gospel and of human resources enables people to handle their common failures constructively. Human suffering, too, is part of those resources. Human suffering can be punitive, remedial, and redemptive. Biblical stewardship, which calls for the proper custodianship of the resources of the Word and of human resources, brings these two together enabling people who are suffering to handle their "share of hardship" constructively through God's grace.[11]

Christian stewardship also focuses on our possessions. In this era, how we make and use our money is an acid test of Christian character. The level of a congregation's giving reveals much about that congregation's commitment to and understanding of the gospel of Jesus Christ. Elementally, Christian stewardship teaches us that we are to love people and use possessions rather than use people and love possessions. Responsible church councils will probe into this truth quite specifically in their study sessions.

Obviously — but it was not obvious to most church people until Rachel Carson and others got at it—biblical stewardship focuses on the care of the earth: land, air, oceans, rivers, lakes, animal and plant life, and so on. We can only say here that while a majority of church people have exploited the resources of the good earth for selfish purposes, there have been some church people who exercise a responsible stewardship of the earth. One of the strands in the Genesis story is clear-cut on that. The other, admittedly, allows for confusion. But Dr. Lynn White's sweeping attack on Christianity for fostering the exploitation of the earth is far afield of reality. Nonetheless, this aspect of stewardship should be delved into seriously in study groups. Meantime, some constructive steps can be taken immediately by everyone in the congregation —curtailed use of energy, altered eating habits, recycling of materials, participation in environmental causes and action groups, and much more.

There is another significant aspect to developing a biblical theology of stewardship: teaching church members to be responsible citizens. This responsibility is especially pressing in a political society that allows for open criticism of government policies, primary and general elections, and secret balloting. Belatedly, the church did play a limited role in the thrust for civil rights legislation in the mid-1960s. It has been exceptionally quiet of late! Looking hard-eyed at the institutionalization of evil in South Africa, and oppression in Russia, Central Europe, Africa, China, Southeast Asia, Brazil, and Chile, many clergy and some lay people are beginning to understand that a proper stewardship of the gospel calls them to a larger concern for human rights in all parts of the world. Here, the church is still part of the problem, not yet part of the answer. It has much land to be possessed in its own ranks. A distinct limitation of the church's credibility in its peripatetic involvements in technical, economic, and political issues is its weak base of support at the grass roots—in short, the hypocrisy of its constituency. The church fails more often than not to practice what it preaches to society.

The church in America has to learn how to draw apart from the world to discern freshly the Word of the Lord, and how to work more honestly to reflect the mind of Christ before it can expect to witness and work effectively in the world.

Certainly, a distinctive Christian life-style set deep in personal commitment to Christ will not emerge among a majority of church members until they understand and do biblical stewardship. Until that majority experiences first-hand the forgiveness and renewing power of Jesus Christ in their lives, they will not exercise a proper custodianship of the Word of God, a responsible care of persons, or an intelligent ecological concern. In baptism, God accepts us into his family. But we must mature as Christian persons, accept a responsible place in the corporate fellowship of Christ, and practice personal discipline in the faith (study of the scriptures, prayer, generous giving, daily witnessing), if we expect people in the world to listen to the good news. This, too, is part of our Christian stewardship.

But to take biblical stewardship seriously and do it in God's strength is to collide with members in one's own congregation and with neighbors, friends, and associates in the world. Specifically, this means that the congregation that seeks to do stewardship biblically comes into conflict with social-economic-political institutions (city, state, and federal governments), some business corporations, and some community social service agencies; the "American" economic philosophy; and fellow-citizens whose life-styles are dictated by unregenerate ego needs. It also means that *that* congregation will collide with some objectives and practices of the institutional church itself. Often, the dictum here, too, is "go along—to get along." The institutional church, influenced strongly by contemporary culture and preoccupied with its institutional needs—like all the institutions of society—gets caught up in managing people, and at worst, manipulating them. That is true in every corner of the church in America, because large numbers of parish pastors and church councils are themselves trying to manage and manipulate people to achieve congregational goals.

Biblical stewardship is neither management nor manipulation. It is confrontation. The Word of God confronts human beings where they are; it calls them to turn away from their ego-centered lives, and to follow Christ without regard for reputation, economic security, or immediate personal satisfactions. Biblical stewardship has Christ's cross at its center. Biblical stewards, exercising their freedom, are willing servants of God's Word. Most congregations in America and Europe, with exceptions here and there, do not think of themselves as servants of the Word. They think of themselves parochially, denominationally, confessionally, sociologically.

For almost thirty years I have been privileged to serve God and people in and through the Lutheran Church of the Holy Trinity, Lancaster, Pennsylvania. During these years we have never set mechanical (statistical) objectives: to increase our income by twelve or twenty percent in any given year; to sponsor an attendance crusade in church or school; or to "get" a defined number of new members in Lent or any other season. Instead, we set *these* objectives which defined our purpose:

• to preach biblically (that is, to set before

people in relevant cultural images and the idiom of the day the *demands* and the *promises* of God)

• to teach evangelical truth and its ethic (life-style)

• to assemble regularly around the Word in preaching and teaching and sacraments

• to learn and do biblical stewardship

• to equip people to witness for Christ in the world in person-to-person evangelism and through specific social means designed to enlarge justice for all people.

This, we judge, is our reasonable service to God. True, we have not become a mighty institution, but our people, fed and cared for from God's Word, have become a powerful Christian presence in Lancaster—and beyond. Some will find our objectives too broad. They *can* be framed more specifically, but they cannot be taken for granted—ever. They are elemental. They reflect the nature and purpose of Christ's church in the world.

Disastrously, the church in America has "committed," "programmed," "emergency appealed," and "social actioned" itself to death, nagging its members for special dollars for this and that, carping on society's misdeeds, playing with liturgies as ends in themselves, majoring in minors, and examining its institutional traumas ad nauseam. Consequently, it is always playing catch-up dollar stewardship, catch-up evangelism, catch-up everything —never willing to risk its life on anything. This short-sighted stewardship, unbiblical to the core, is like our nation's current helter-skelter thrusts at a sane energy program and like the major powers' tinkering with nuclear arms control. But we Christians should know better. Jesus said plainly that life must be risked, sacrificed, if it is to be lived in his service. He did not die to give church members an easy peace of mind or to relieve their consciences through a five hundred-dollar single gift to the church. He died to liberate men and women *from* sin and death *for* life in his service. There is an elemental sense in which critical-minded, concerned church members give generously to and through "their" congregation because they know first-hand that "their" congregation *is* a little corner of God's own kingdom, leaven in "their" secular community, daringly active on the frontiers of secular life and thought.

The authentic steward allows God's Word to confront his or her person and speaks God's truth in love to others. People are free to decide what they will; some will say yes; others will say no. The Rich Young Ruler went away sorrowing. That was not Jesus' fault. One thief on Calvary died alone. That was not Jesus' failure to care. Nine

healed lepers went selfishly on their way; that was
not Jesus' fault. Judas, heartbroken and *unable to
redeem himself*, turned away from Christ and
hanged himself. That was not Jesus' fault. Zacchaeus decided to practice a sweeping kind of
stewardship. That happened because, in his freedom, Zacchaeus accepted Jesus' gift of friendship.
The widow gave her mite because, in her freedom,
she placed God above her own comfort, convenience, and security.

The pastor(s), church council, and members of
each congregation decide for themselves whether
they will grow in Christ or be stunted as persons
because they treat his demands and promises cava-
lierly. The proper stewardship of God's Word is to
let it confront you and me and others. Truth
spoken in love does not violate human freedom.
Coercion does. Manipulation does. Management
does. Truth spoken in love is God's way of dealing
with human prodigals. The church simply must
try it more often! The last estate of people who
"play church" is worse than the first. Disregard
for God's radical Word is the one unpardonable
sin, because the Holy Spirit works mediately
through his Word.

• Congregations that are loyal to Christ have a
word to Russia and Western Europe and the United
States because these, more than others, are engaged

presently in a nuclear arms race that threatens humanity itself.

• Christ's church has a specific word to the leaders of South Africa who have institutionalized evil.

• Christ's church has a word to its own members who, with their fellow-citizens in America, comprise six percent of the world's population yet use forty percent of the earth's resources.

• Christ's church in America will ask its teenagers whether it is morally responsible to tool around in automobiles when the energy crisis is deepening. (Western European nations and Japan have asked the United States pointedly to practice energy conservation as they do themselves.)

• Christ's church will ask its members whether they, and other Americans, have the moral right to use precious grain to fatten beef to place steaks on millions of tables when ten thousand human beings die each day from starvation.

• Christ's church will also ask more specific questions like these:

   —Do middle-class church members who have a comfortable home, two cars, and a bundle of luxuries have the right to cry, "Lord, Lord," on Sunday, place six to eight left-over dollars on the offering plate weekly and live the other six days of the week under other gods, yet ask the blessing of God in their lives? Is that stewardship or hypocrisy?

—Does any middle-class congregation in America have the moral right to live comfortably while keeping its clergy and other church employees at a level of genteel poverty?

—Does any church member have the right to accept election to the church council, if he or she contributes only the leftovers from a solid income, worships sporadically, evangelizes rarely, and fails to open the Bible from one month to the next?

Specific questions like these bring the broad descriptions of biblical stewardship down where the church exists: the local congregation.

Here is another complex question that emerges in doing biblical stewardship. Does any congregation that exists by the skin of its teeth in a community that is overchurched have the right to place over ninety percent of its annual budget into a ministry that is in fact a private chaplaincy to a handful. My own view, after a quarter of a century of meeting with clergy of all denominations and some sects in several hundred conferences, is that upwards of a fifth, perhaps more, of the congregations now in existence are "unfaithful stewards" in seeking to keep their doors open rather than joining selflessly with another congregation or two to provide a full ministry to their members and community, and, through the church-at-large, the nation and world. In some congregations, this is the first stewardship question that needs to be asked, discussed openly and honestly, and decided under the guidance of the Holy Spirit.

In evaluating the different aspects of the congregation's life, responsible stewards will ask periodically whether the pastoral leadership of the church is effective *and* whether the lay members of the church are engaged in a ministry that distinguishes the church from other social institutions. Each pastor has the right and the obligation as a steward, to discuss candidly and good-spiritedly with the church council whether his or her salary is equitable, his or her housing comfortable, his or her allowance for books and periodicals and continuing education adequate. An especially difficult part of learning to do biblical stewardship is for the pastor *and* the elected lay leaders to examine humbly not only their own giving patterns but also their motives for giving. Each member of the church is responsible before God for the maturity of his giving level whether the pastor or lay leaders act responsibly or not. The reality is, however, that church members overmatch budgets first because they love the Lord and people, second because they understand biblical stewardship, third because "their" congregation is engaged with life as it is lived in the world, and fourth because the ordained and lay leaders provide them with mature examples, even as they themselves are called to be Christ-bearers in the world.

It is in these temporal, mundane areas that a congregation's stewardship proves its biblical character. The Word of God is always concrete and specific. If the pastor and lay leaders cannot discuss stewardship concretely and specifically among themselves, they are not equipped to go to their fellow-church members asking them to be responsible stewards. Biblical stewardship begins with the pastor(s) and lay leaders in the local congregation or it is not likely to begin at all.

For Discussion

1. The church's primary act of stewardship is its proper custodianship of God's Word in preaching and teaching and sacraments. What then is the responsibility of the elected representatives of our congregation for its custodianship? In what sense, if any, is responsible biblical scholarship a part of our congregation's custodianship of God's Word?

2. If you were to state in a single sentence what the heart of the gospel is, what would you say? When is the preaching and teaching in a congregation "cheap grace"? When is it "shallow moralism"? When is it corporately and/or personally self-indulgent? When is it the "full counsel of God?"

3. Are the lay leaders in our congregation's church school serving under a "call" to teach the doctrine of the Word that the congregation's denomination espouses? How are the lay teachers in our church school equipped to be effective teachers of evangelical truth? What do we expect our school's pupils to learn? Believe? Do?

4. Should the church council discuss openly with the pastor the content of his or her preaching and teaching? Allowing that the Word of God is preached and taught intelligibly and persuasively in our congregation, do the church council members attempt to *act* on that preaching and teaching on the other six days of the week? Do our members? Discuss.

5. If indeed the church was bought for a price and for a purpose, how do we define our congregation's purpose in our community? Denomination? Nation? World?

6. What is the evangelistic work of a Christian congregation? Does Christian evangelism have social as well as personal implications? What is person-to-person evangelism? Is there, in fact, a Christian life-style? If so, outline its shape from biblical sources.

7. Does our congregation see its life in terms of concentric circles — membership, persons in the neighborhood, people in our metropolitan or rural area, citizens in the nation, people in the world? If so, in what specific ways?

8. Is there a *Christian* stewardship of the self? Discuss.

9. Is there evident tension between our congregation and the community in which we worship and witness?

10. Looking back over the last quarter century, what did our church do about the "McCarthy virus" in the early 1950s? Nuclear testing in the mid-1950s and after? The religious question in the Kennedy-Nixon campaign of 1960? The Cuban missile crisis, 1962? Civil rights in *our* community during the 1960s, and presently? The Vietnam War? Watergate? World hunger? Poverty? Human rights in Russia, Brazil, Chile, South Korea, Cambodia, the United States?

11. In what ways is our community aware of our congregation's presence? The pulpit? Corporate community involvement? Political involvement? Leadership of our members in the secular arena? Corporately, do we have a voice that is heard with *respect* in our community? Does our congregation make the *right* enemies for Christ's sake? The church council may want to provide a forum for the congregation in addressing and discussing these questions posed by biblical stewardship.

4

DOLLAR
STEWARDSHIP

A S PART OF GOD'S CREATION, Christians
are stewards of his gifts. They are called
and appointed by Christ to manage
"their" material goods responsibly. In the biblical
sense, how we use our material possessions is as
important as how we come to possess them. Jesus
taught that God had pronounced his creation
good and looked upon that goodness with satis-
faction. Jesus did not draw a distinction between
material goods as "evil" and spirituality as "good."
In offering himself for the pardon of our sins, he
demonstrated that responsible stewardship em-
braces all areas of human existence. Christ-followers are not "souls with ears." They are embodied
spirits who live in this world.

In his teachings, Jesus demonstrated again and
again his concern that all people have the oppor-

tunity to participate fully in the goodness of God's material creation as well as in spiritual communion with him. It is the unredeemed human attitude that is the barrier to a responsible use of wealth. Selfish desires and insensitive attitudes serve the best interests of no one. But Jesus did not identify material goods as evil. He did not direct Zacchaeus to divest himself of all his possessions when he saw that the "new" Zacchaeus was using them to serve others in need. When we surrender to God's will for us, we are enabled to use our possessions in the interest of others. So, through the ages, Christ-followers have sought to serve God with their material wealth, falteringly to be sure, yet deliberately and hopefully.[12]

We said at the outset that stewardship is corporate and personal. It is the responsibility of Christian congregations as well as Christian individuals. But building a budget, presenting it to the congregation, the mechanics of receiving pledges and offerings, the keeping of financial records, and the distribution of the monies received according to the budget are responsibilities of the official board. Most church councils delegate these specific responsibilities to their finance and stewardship committees. Normally, a congregation has committees for evangelism, stewardship, worship and music, parish education, finance, property, and an executive committee. Large congregations, especially those involved in community ministries, have in addition to these, committees for social ministry, social action, the study of social issues, internal benevolence, staff relationships, trusts and endowments, investments, and special purposes. In many congregations, council members serve as the chairpersons of large committees comprised of other council members as well as members from the congregation. This gives the congregation a larger voice in decision-making. Of course, large committees require competent chairpersons. That is part of stewardship, too. The clergy need not attend all the meetings of all committees unless the parish is in a crisis situation. Ordinarily, the pastor (and other clergy in staff ministries) serves as staff liaison or consultant for several committees. A proper stewardship of time does not allow the clergy to do what lay people can do as well or better.

The stewardship committee's *primary* responsibility is *not* the supervision of a particular year's pledging. The stewardship committee exists to see that biblical stewardship is taught in the church council, leadership schools for lay teachers, and open meetings throughout the congregation year in and year out. This work is never done. In congregations that call forward mature Christians as lay leaders, the church council itself is a committee of the whole that oversees the teaching and doing of stewardship and evangelism.

The following model works effectively, but it is not the only model that is effective. The finance committee, preparing the budget for the coming year, will ask the chairpersons of all committees in May of each year to convene their committees during the next several months to examine the work for which they are responsible, appraise how it has been done since the preceding September, and determine what monies will be needed for the coming year. These committees are expected to do their work seriously, not perfunctorily, and make clear-headed recommendations to the finance committee by August. These estimates, carefully framed, are reviewed by the finance committee in early September when the full budget is constructed. This carefully prepared budget is then presented to the church council two months before Stewardship Sunday. The board accepts the budget as presented or modifies it. This council-approved budget is mimeographed or printed and mailed to all the members of the congregation. It is then discussed and approved (sometimes with amendments) at a congregational meeting. Instead of a congregational meeting, some congregations provide sessions after the Sunday worship services so that the members of the congregation can examine and question any part of the budget in person-to-person meetings with members of the stewardship and finance committees. The actual budget for the congregation is determined *after* the pledging. If the approved budget is under-pledged, the church council will make proper reductions as a matter of integrity. If the budget is over-pledged, as it regularly is in congregations where biblical stewardship is taught, the council will restore cuts made in September to committees which had asked for larger allocations. Where there is a large over-subscription, the congregation is invited to identify benevolence objectives for the distribution of these additional monies. So much for the budget, except to say that responsible church councils expend monies as the congregationally-approved pledged budget allows. A congregation that pays benevolence monies after doing everything for itself has little to say to its members who give what is "left-over" after satisfying their ego needs.

Here are some things that ought *not* to be done and some things that *ought* to be done. These suggestions reflect my own quarter century of teaching biblical stewardship in a congregation of 1700 communicants (650 families) that has moved steadily from a $40,000 annual expenditure (one-fourth for benevolence) to a $510,000 annual expenditure (one-half for benevolence) while providing another three and a half million dollars to build a parish house, replace a four manual organ, and renovate its historic sanctuary twice.

DO NOT inflate the budget or provide a "safety factor" even though you inform the people that this has been done. Such a budget is unrealistic, confusing, potentially dishonest.

DO NOT provide three budgets — minimum, limited advance, and strong advance. This is mechanical and manipulative. Let it be said plainly that an honestly-drawn budget should be over-matched, and it will be in time, if the members are taught biblical stewardship. Annual pledging provides a specific occasion—certainly, not the only occasion — for motivating individual members to mature as Christian people in their understanding and practice of "dollar" stewardship.

If an every-member visitation is employed, DO NOT select careless givers as visitors. Do not select visitors who gossip or sympathize with people who criticize the clergy and lay leadership *unfairly*. Responsible criticisms should be heard and shared with the pastor and church council. Do not select visitors who have no sense of the church beyond their own doors.

DO NOT expend the congregation's energies by over-preparing for the visitations. Where biblical stewardship is taught throughout the year a half hour's "briefing" is adequate.

Now, some things that ought to be done.

First, before Stewardship Sunday, the congregation should be advised of the weekly and annual amounts pledged by the pastor(s) and the members of the church council—*without names.* These pledges will be made two months in advance at the council meeting at which the budget is approved— and following candid discussion among the clergy and council members. If this cannot be done, the church council is the first place where teaching biblical stewardship must begin. This is, even after twenty-eight years, a task I shrink from. But it is one of the pastor's teaching responsibilities. Until the ordained and elected lay leaders of a congregation are themselves persuaded by the gospel and the evidences of human need in this world to do generous, proportionate, and disciplined giving, it is not likely that the congregation (except for a family here and there) will give really serious thought to a biblical stewardship of their possessions. The bland can lead the bland, but only to be more bland. It is maturing stewards of the gospel —alert in their custodianship of the Word; responsive to the needs of persons in the congregation, community, and the world; active in their care of the earth; and persuaded to exercise a stewardship of the self, including possessions—who teach others biblical stewardship and encourage them to practice it.

The elected lay leaders of the congregation and the congregation itself have a right to expect a mature understanding and generous practice of dollar stewardship by their pastor(s). Equally, the pastor(s) and the congregation have a right to expect their elected lay leaders to study, learn, and do biblical stewardship. Those council members who are *not willing to grow* in doing stewardship and evangelism ought, as an act of simple integrity, to surrender their positions to other persons (perhaps less well-known in the community) who *are* maturing in the faith. The awful truth is that uncommitted church members have been making a shambles or a mockery of stewardship and evangelism in mainline Protestant churches for the last quarter of a century.

As I have pointed out in other books on the life and work of the parish, criteria should be established for nominating men and women to be elected to the church council.[13] These are the criteria that Trinity's Vestry defined twenty years ago. Each nominee for vestry shall be a *regular* participant in the worship services and *active* in Christian education. Each shall be an *active* evangelist. Each shall be *maturing* in his or her dollar stewardship.

Each shall be able to make decisions for the *whole* congregation rather than for the handful of members he or she knows best. Electing people to the church council simply because they are large contributors, or because they are influential in the community, or because they are eager for the position, or because the office has to be filled, is a flagrant violation of biblical stewardship. How can unconverted men and women oversee the preaching and teaching of God's Word and the proper administration of the sacraments? How can they lead a community of people who promised to seek and do God's will? If a congregation cannot call forward twelve, fifteen, twenty, or thirty men and women (whatever the complement of the official board may be), that congregation, seeking to exercise responsible stewardship, must ask whether it has a right to function as a congregation. Until laypeople begin to look honestly at *their* place of pastoral leadership in the church and the place of their congregation in the community, thousands of Protestant congregations will be led by church people who sign themselves to Christ, "Casually yours."

Second, take a firm stand on pledging. It is still necessary in some congregations to point out that no *member* has the right to decline to sign a pledge. The member who says, "I don't believe in pledging," needs to be challenged person-to-person.

Almost without exception, this response is a dodge that allows members to contribute little to the church they promised to support when they promised their fellow-members, themselves, and God to follow Christ. This should be said plainly by the pastor(s) and lay leaders alike. Confrontation-in-freedom is the style of Christian ministry. Speaking God's truth in love on all matters of faith and life to others *and* hearing it spoken by others to us is a basic strand in the church's Christian witness in the world and its pastoral care of people.

Third, the church council will explain clearly to the members that a pledge to the church is an act of faith, not a legal obligation. They will make it plain that any member can and should adjust his or her pledge upward or downward to reflect any substantial change in his or her income or family responsibilities in the course of any year.

Fourth, if an every-member visitation is employed, the council and the pastor(s) are responsible for choosing mature stewards who can and will sit down for a forty-five minute discussion of the life and work of the church and biblical giving in each home visited. Visitors who do not give responsibly will say after a few minutes of casual conversation, "Just put down whatever you want to give." This kind of visitation is a waste of time and energy. It is hurtful to persons and the congregation. It is an offense to the crucified God.

Fifth, in those congregations that pledge at worship services, council members will be present at all services. Some congregations overmatch their budget at these services on a single Sunday. Most, however, designate two or three consecutive Sundays for their erratic attenders and then visit those who have not pledged. A few churches in America, reaching into the Judeo-Christian tradition, function on annual covenants made by their members: those who sign pledges are considered active members for the coming year. Some church councils may want to examine this kind of stewardship. It is *not* our practice at Trinity Church.

But these are means. There are others. Bazaars, congregational dinners, and street fairs should be held for fellowship, not fund raising. Generally speaking, cards calling for pledges of time and talent for church and community work should not be mixed with pledges for giving money. This "talent" aspect of pledging should be done at another time. It is effective in some congregations, a waste of time in others.

At this point I would like to set down, but not discuss, several judgments about trusts and endowments. (1) Until a congregation is doing biblical stewardship a "trust fund" is a liability. (2) When

a congregation's mind is oriented to the use of
monies for persons, a trust fund can be administered so that God's work is done through it.
(3) The income from such a fund should be usable
as the church council sees fit rather than locked
to narrow, irrelevant purposes. (4) Trust monies
should not be invested in corporations or utilities
that directly violate human rights[14] Some responsible church people are convinced that congregations should not have endowment funds. This is
an honorable view among Christians, but it is open
to debate on biblical grounds. The preceding four
judgments on endowment funds can be taken as
discussion points in church councils.

Finally, in any serious consideration of "dollar"
stewardship, church councils will study carefully
the tithe in Christian giving. *Voluntary tithing* is a
legitimate means for fostering a Christian stewardship of money. But in employing it, one needs to
recall the basic uses of the law in Christian context. Jesus did not destroy the law; he fulfilled it.
We must face the reality that all Christians need
the law for restraint, for guidance, and as a mirror
that reflects their growth in Christ. God's laws are
"commands with promise." [15] While God-in-Christ
has set us free from judgment under the law, we
still need the restraint and guidance of the law. We
should not grow weary in well-doing, but we do.

Paul did. Peter, deep into the faith, still sought a final reward as his *due* for "having forsaken all." Discipline-in-freedom is part of authentic Christian growth.

There is no evidence that Jesus ever asked anyone directly to tithe. It does appear, however, that he, a devout Hebrew, tithed. Paul urged his fellow-Christians quite bluntly to give (a) as the Lord had prospered them, (b) regularly, (c) weekly, and (d) proportionately (1 Cor. 16:21; 2 Cor. 8:11-14). The New Testament view of giving does not eliminate the voluntary tithe as one form of disciplined, proportionate giving, even as God's gospel does not eliminate his moral law. Christians are *new* creatures, but they are still *creatures,* disposed to do things they ought not to do and indisposed to do those things they ought to do. Justification is not sanctification. Christians—members of God's family by his grace and their personal decision—do not become fully responsible family members in this present life.

The voluntary tithe — disciplined giving by choice — should be prayerfully considered and thoroughly discussed by affluent middle and upper-class church members as a necessary discipline in their Christian lives. Affluence, the by-product of a technological society and fortuitous (providential) circumstances, is easily mishandled. The Rich Young Ruler, the well-to-do farmer who built new barns on the eve of his unexpected death, and middle and upper-class American people are ugly proofs of that. Affluence, presently out of control in more than half of our American homes, damages persons and society as John Galbraith pointed out two decades ago in one of the most significant books published since World War II, *The Affluent Society*. After the mid-1950s, a similar and interrelated affluence in West Germany, Japan, and the oil-producing Arab States, linked with ours, has upset the world economy. On a planet where mass starvation and galloping inflation are grim realities the moral implications of concentrated affluence are plainly evident.

In our country, this affluence breeds envy, covetousness, and greed. The family with one car wants to be like the next door neighbors who have two cars. The family with two cars and two children in their late teens wants three or four cars. Private transportation is a must in our society, but it does not require a family fleet, or Mercedes-Benz, Cadillac Seville, and Lincoln Continental autos. Our affluence, resting now on the shaky economy of uncritical consumerism, built-in obsolescence, and surging inflation, must be handled sensibly, sensitively, *and* quickly. Otherwise, government controls will come and, with them, their own peculiar evils. Our present affluence breeds an unconscious selfishness in the face of grave human needs in the world. Out of control, it inspires an unhealthy competitiveness that is fed by undisciplined ego needs which in turn produce conflict in the family, the church, between classes, among races, and between nations. Affluence run wild, breeds self-reliance rather than God-reliance. Of course, widespread poverty, which exists in part because of an irresponsible affluence, also breeds the same sins that affluence breeds—envy, covetousness, greed, frustration, anger, violence.

Tithing as a voluntary act of personal discipline (obedience-in-freedom) — linked with disciplined worship, Bible study, prayer, and witness—invites serious consideration by middle and upper-class church members who presently have more than they need. Personally and vocationally, I am committed to tithing. Clarence Stoughton, lay director of the former United Lutheran Church in America's Office of Stewardship, persuaded me in the first years of my ministry with the simple statement: "Tithing is the first reasonable step in Christian stewardship." I took that then, and still do, as a working guide for doing "dollar" stewardship. My wife and I tithed on $2100 a year, including parsonage, when I began my ministry more than three decades ago. Oriented to community needs by our families, we provided half for the church and half for secular agencies. Taking the tithe as a working guide, our giving has increased propor-

tionately (well beyond a double-tithe) with each
salary increase over the years. Giving proportionately (more than a tithe in tens of thousands of
families) is a moral imperative in our affluent society if Christians want seriously to be truly human and to work with others in fashioning a just
society here and now.[16]

Several qualifying observations about tithing
must be set down. First, in a society where twenty
million people beyond the age of sixty-five live on
inadequate incomes (pensions) and another thirty
million live on welfare grants, it is not possible for
these economically depressed people to tithe. It
would be unchristian to ask *all* church members to
tithe, or triple tithe, even as it was burdensome in
other centuries when the church, by law, imposed
the tithe on all citizens. I have commended the
tithe to comfortable and affluent church members as
an act of obedience-in-freedom, a first reasonable
step in Christian giving, not as a requirement for
participation in the congregation's life and work.

Second, any notion that tithing brings personal
prosperity to the practitioner is contrary to the
gospel and human experience. The Bible sets it
down with jarring candor that the wicked often
prosper and the righteous frequently fail. Any sug-
gestion that tithing is a meritorious deed is unbiblical. Christian giving is voluntary, disciplined,

glad-hearted, sometimes spontaneous. It is a strand in one's personal and corporate participation in Christ's ministry.

> Christian stewardship begins with the existential recognition and acceptance that the servant is not above his Master. Repentance and gospel faith; an expectant waiting on the Holy Spirit; and the humbling of self, congregation, and denomination before God are integral strands in a biblical response to God's grace. Repentance and gospel faith motivate and enable the church to participate in God's stewardship which has a cross at the center of it.[17]

For Discussion

1. If our congregation cannot provide at least a quarter of its total income for benevolence objectives, care responsibly for its own members from birth to death, and attract new members from all age brackets, economic levels, and races, are we doing biblical stewardship?

2. Should our pastor speak about money from the pulpit, in board meetings, in some counseling situations, and in home visits? Why? Why not?

3. Does our congregation, or our pastor, entertain any notions that discussions about money violate the nature of the gospel?

4. Others have pointed out that Jesus spoke five times more often about material holdings than about prayer. Confirm this observation biblically and discuss its implications for our church and community.

5. The gospel accounts make it clear that Jesus gave his primary—but not exclusive—attention to the dispossessed, the demonically possessed, the physically disabled, the sorrowing, and the oppressed. To whom and what does the ministry (full-time and lay) of our congregation give its primary attention? What are our priorities?

6. Does our official board discuss its own pledging and then proceed to overmatch their fair shares of the budgets they have constructed? Are all the members of our official board maturing stewards of their earthly goods? Are there Christian criteria for evaluating a responsible and irresponsible stewardship of "possessions"? What are they? Should the pastor and official board advise the congregation prior to the annual pledging what they have pledged and why (without names)? Discuss.

7. It has been observed often since the early 1960s that one of the major hypocrisies in the contemporary church is the difference between what it says about the stewardship of material goods and how it practices stewardship. Is that true of our congregation?

8. As the wheat and the tares grow together in the church, and as the disciples of Jesus represented a closer association with him than the crowds who followed him, do we agree or disagree with the argument in this chapter that all members of the official board should worship regularly, participate in the church school, evangelize actively, be maturing stewards, and have the ability to decide issues in the interests of the *whole* congregation? Discuss specifically.

9. Do you consider the tithe to be legalistic, a minimal standard for individual giving, or a stumbling block? Discuss.

10. If one tithes or double-tithes or triple-tithes, should one-half of the *total* amount one gives go to secular community agencies that care for persons and/or work for social justice, to educational institutions, and to people's advocates in the state and national governments?

11. Does tithing as a voluntary act of personal discipline enrich the person of the practitioner? Are there any notions in our congregation that tithing brings personal prosperity to the practitioner? Discuss these two questions fully, distinguishing clearly between them.

5

EXPLOSIVE
QUESTIONS ON
BIBLICAL STEWARDSHIP

WHAT BELONGS TO GOD; what belongs to the state? This double-pronged question may become the most stubborn, disruptive stewardship question that Christians face in the last two decades of this century. We would not presume to suggest — other than to underscore Jesus' clear-cut directive on giving to God what belongs rightfully to him and to the state what belongs properly to it—how church members in Czechoslovakia or Poland, Yugoslavia or Russia, Brazil or Chile should answer these questions.

But in America we have a radically different political situation guaranteed by law. Article Six of the American Constitution reads: "No religious test shall ever be required as a qualification to any office of public trust under the United States." No constitutional law disbarred Alfred E. Smith, Roman Catholic, from running for President in 1928, or John F. Kennedy, Roman Catholic, from running for and being elected President in 1960. The Federal law allows any citizen of stated age, whatever his or her creed, color, sex, or class may be, to run for any federal office. Deep-seated prejudices in society disallow this or that person being elected to office, or even being nominated, but the law of the land does not.

Further, the First Amendment to the Constitution declares that Congress shall not interfere with the freedoms of press, speech, religion, assembly, or the right to petition. This means, in the context of our discussion, that any religious body in America is free to disseminate its views, lobby, and, in other legitimate ways, bring its point of view (values, convictions) to bear on candidacies and government policies. There was considerable friction—and some illegal acts by the government—over the First Amendment (freedom of religion, speech, press, assembly, and petition) during the 1960s and early 1970s. But the law was not changed. A corps of church members, together with unchurched people concerned over civil rights, influenced the government to enact civil rights legislation and to "winddown" the war in Vietnam. The view, voiced often in church circles, that the church should not speak to social-economic-political issues is contrary to

the American Constitution. It is contrary to past
American experience, especially in the eighteenth
and nineteenth centuries. *It is contrary to biblical
faith.*

Some of the intellectual stimulus for enacting
the First Amendment, especially on the separation
of church and state, came from Thomas Jefferson.
He was the author of the Statute of Religious Freedom for Virginia in 1786, which was in turn in-
corporated into the Federal Constitution and the
First Amendment. But Jefferson supported and fos-
tered the view that church members (citizens of
the nation) would and should address those political
and social issues which concerned them.[18] This kind
of direct and indirect influence was exerted steadily
during the nineteenth century (against slavery, the
Mexican War, corporations, holding companies, the
rape of natural resources, child labor, the subjuga-
tion of women, and so on). Responsible church-
manship as well as responsible citizenship requires
each Christian to bring his or her views to bear on
elections, domestic policies, international diplo-
macy, foreign alliances, trade agreements, immigra-
tion policies, nuclear armaments, and other issues
of the day.

Strangely, some church members who support
lobbying by the National Rifle Association or by
groups opposed to legal abortion argued against and
often vilified other church members who lobbied

and marched for civil rights legislation in the early 1960s and opposed the Vietnam War. Many Protestants and Roman Catholics are decidedly less objective and informed citizens in our political society than many unchurched citizens. Christians who do not seek to bring their understanding of God's will to bear on broad domestic and international issues are disobedient to Jesus' directive to give to God what belongs to him. They are also irresponsible citizens since the health of a republic depends on the enlightened, moral involvement of its citizens in public forums where conflicting views are aired and in general elections where they are decided.

The issue of church and state, Christ and culture, is an old chestnut in medieval and modern European history. It is a vibrantly alive issue in America today. It will become more so in the closing years of this century. H. Richard Niebuhr calls this centuries-old struggle, "the double wrestle of the church with its Lord and with the cultural society with which it lives." Oscar Cullmann, Lutheran biblical scholar, concluded a quarter of a century ago that, "the question of Church and State is so closely bound up with the gospel itself that they emerge together." [19]

American Christians who want to exercise a proper stewardship of the gospel, a responsible care for people in the world, and an enlightened custodianship of the earth's resources will

- learn to accept the world as God's creation

- face the reality that politics in a republic is one means to create a more humane society and define policies that lead to peace in the world

- get free of their simplistic views of the relationship between Christ and culture, accept and face complex political issues, and seek to transform and structure positively the ambiguous interactions between church and state

- bring knowledge, wisdom, integrity, and courage to bear on political decision-making in a society which guarantees by law their right to do so

- seek to discern God at work in the ambiguities of contemporary history as well as the ambiguities of biblical history.

This is also a basic responsibility of biblical scholarship, theology, and preaching. Together, these make up a solid part of *biblical* stewardship.

If American Christians are to exercise a responsible stewardship of the gospel, they must learn quickly to demand through their elected representatives that this nation's foreign policy reflect what they proclaim: Christ loves all people. Christianity is supranational. The issue is not only church and state; it is also church and *states*. Christians will be concerned not only about human rights at home but also about human rights in Russia and China, Brazil and Chile, India and South Africa. "The Church," Allen Geyer reminds us, "has a transnational life which touches a vast plurality of states."

Luther's celebrated but widely misunderstood doctrine of the two kingdoms provides enlightenment and guidance for those who understand the doctrine, take it seriously, and handle it imaginatively. Simply put, Luther, like Augustine, saw the church and state existing in tension. Every Christian has obligations to *both* institutions of society. But his or her first allegiance is to God, not to country or party or race or creed or sex. The Christian's active witness may or may not alter the course of a secular state, but each Christian is obligated nonetheless to make his or her witness. To be specific: President Carter's statement about human rights in Russia is in accord with the Helsinki Agreement into which the Soviet Union freely entered. But apart from that agreement, President Carter, a professing Christian, is obligated to speak out. *How* he speaks and *how* he brings his views to bear on this human issue are open to discussion and debate.[20] But, as a professing Christian, he must speak and act. So must we. Human rights, rooted in human dignity, is a biblical concept.

Only the small Confessing Church in Germany (Barmen Declaration of 1934) and a minority of

Roman Catholics spoke out against Nazi persecution and efforts to liquidate the Jews. Had the
Christian church risen in force in Germany in 1933
when Hitler assumed power unconstitutionally—
or even as late as the Crystal Night in 1938—the
holocaust could have been averted. If the American
church had spoken strongly against the Vietnam
War in 1964, the economic condition of this nation
would be more stable, its conscience less troubled,
and several million human lives would have been
saved. If, in the early decades of the nineteenth century, the church in the South and the North had
spoken firmly against the immoral practice of en-
slaving black human beings, the tragedy, the chaos,
and the ill will that still mark black-white rela-
tions might have been averted in this nation. The
mainline Protestant and Roman Catholic churches,
critical of privatistic religion in the 1970s, are
themselves guilty of fostering the same heresy
among their members. In fact, many preach a
privatistic religion; they endorse people's current
flight from freedom, their escape from social responsibility, their pursuit of loneliness.

Consider, for example, this random list of current and emerging issues of church and state: abortion, genetic engineering, public welfare, national
health insurance, social security, an equitable tax
structure, military spending, limitation of nuclear
arms, energy, internal security (invasion of pri-

vacy), control of the news media (presently, the sponsor), civil religion, religious use of the communications media, firearms control, penal reform, international conglomerates, public and private education, care of the aging, world-wide poverty and mass starvation, population control, the emerging third and fourth worlds, armaments sales, and so on. Each of these is a moral-social-political issue which the church will address and act on in concert with other concerned citizens *if* it takes the stewardship of God's Word seriously.[21]

All the major political and economic issues facing American society today are moral issues. The ethical decisions that Christians must make in politics and business, as well as in the realm of private relationships, are an essential strand in biblical stewardship. The American church is not and cannot be apolitical. The doctrine of separation of church and state neither constrains nor suggests that the church be isolated from the political tides and undercurrents of our pluralistic society. Of course, this would be impossible in any case. The actions and policies of government are influenced by well-organized and well-heeled lobbies and by the concerned and concerted efforts of private citizens. The real issue to be decided then is whether the church will act responsibly in the realm of politics and economics or whether it will turn in upon itself with the justification of "serving our own."

In spite of these realities, the stewardship materials produced by American Protestants to date scarcely touch this aspect of biblical stewardship. A decade ago, Joseph Fletcher observed that the stewardship presented in the materials of the Protestant churches was condescending, manipulative, and parochial. The American church concentrates its appeals for money on meeting ecclesiastical needs and programs and sharing "with the less fortunate." This provides church members with a vague sort of spiritual indulgence. Consequently, it fosters the unbiblical and destructive view that Christian stewardship is confined to the life of the church and its programs, not to the issues that affect human beings in our complex secular society. In seeking to meet its financial goals, the church has produced few serious and comprehensive studies of fiscal policy, investment practice, or economic theory. A more thoughtful, enlightened, and thorough approach is needed now if this field is to be broadened. This will test the church's willingness to do biblical stewardship.[22]

Perhaps the most pressing church-state question in the 1980s will turn out to be (for the church) not genetic engineering, human rights, world hunger, abortion, or arms control, but whether the state has the right to tax further the church. Most churches, largely unconverted and accustomed to a position of privilege, will become deeply involved in this issue *because of their self-interest.* That has been the most powerful lever in the church's political activities to date—self-interest. The Amish objected when the state sought to educate their children. The peace churches were politically active in opposing the Vietnam War. Evangelicals in some quarters still agitate for Bible reading and Christian prayer in the public schools. The Roman Catholic church, joined by right to life Protestants, has marshaled its forces to attack the Supreme Court's decision that makes abortion legal. The church *is* political when its self-interest is at stake, yet strangely (sinfully) apolitical when its institutional interests are benefited or not hurt by the state. This reality is another damning piece of evidence that the church does not do biblical stewardship.

Back to taxes! Presently, the total tax burden on most American citizens is heavy and, in many cases, inequitable. Billions of tax dollars are used irresponsibly not only for armaments and corporate subsidies but also for public welfare and education. It appears that tax reform and a broader tax base will be legislated in the coming decade because of popular pressures for it. That is in order. But Christians, as biblical stewards, will work diligently to see that this nation's hard-won gains in social concern are not lost in this process. Extreme self-interest will be the moral issue.

Since the church pays taxes now (local, state,

federal excise taxes, federal transportation tax on travel, and since 1976 federal [corporate income] tax on church-owned businesses which are not related directly to the church's generally accepted mission), and church members pay municipal, state, and federal taxes like their unchurched fellow citizens, the real question is, "How shall the church be taxed?" A direct tax on incomes from all church investments? Property taxes on all church buildings? Elimination of the deductions now allowed all taxpayers for charity giving?

We pose these questions here in the hope that clergy and church councils will dig into some detailed studies on this aspect of the church's stewardship. But even in this brief study, we must single out two specific tax issues which reveal how much the church needs to grow in Christ to do "dollar stewardship" in a biblical style. (1) What would be the effect on charity giving (church, United Fund agencies, private colleges, foundations, and so on) if the federal government disallowed *all* tax exemptions on this kind of giving? (2) How can church members, clergy and laity, criticize honestly the government's subsidies to airlines, corporations, students, and welfare recipients when they approve federal subsidies to all clergy (but not to other church employees) through exemptions on housing allowances and parsonages because they keep down the congregation's "cost" for clergy?

The tax issue for churches is complex. The specific questions are sticky, embarrassing, and revealing. Nonetheless, the tax issue will emerge full blown in the 1980s. It is only *one* among many complex questions in the ambiguous realm of church-state relationships that will come to the fore in the closing decades of this century.

The church's current credibility in social-political issues (and technical and economic issues) is weakened by the lack of grass roots support, by the hypocrisy of its members, and by the church's own failure to practice in its congregations what it preaches to the world. This lack roots in two faults:

(1) most church members are not enlightened on the issues (being concerned about only their own particular field—medicine, law, teaching, business, engineering, plumbing, farming, and so on), and

(2) many lay members—and clergy, too—are not firmly committed to Christ and his ethic. Biblical stewardship calls for the enlightened mind and the compassionate heart. Even more, it calls for the converted will ("not my will, but thine be done").

Stewardship rooted in God's demands and promises calls for daily ethical decisions and deeds—personal and social. These Christian decisions and deeds can be examined for motives, ends, means, and social consequences. To do so regularly is to repent daily, or harden one's heart against God. Since human motives are never pure, maturing Christians will inquire diligently of themselves whether their stewardship is motivated by an urgent desire to bring God's love and justice to others. They will also examine critically the end(s) they perceive God wants advanced in our political society for the sake of persons. These inquiries will lead them to examine not only their own priorities but also the priorities of all social institutions—family, church, education, and government—through which they share their money, gifts, contributions, and taxes. They will also determine whether the means they employ or endorse in these institutions of society are consonant with the gospel. Mechanical devices, legalistic formulas, emotional pitches, and manipulation, all of which encourage class-serving and self-justifying gifts and public services that thwart God's grace, are not biblical stewardship. The church, we observed in Chapter 1, has in the past resorted to unbiblical means for "raising" money. It still does.

The church's effective witness during the remainder of this volcanic century will depend substantially on its rediscovering and shaping its life to the biblical concept of stewardship. At the same time, it must stand firmly against a secular, industrial, and technological society that both reflects and feeds our nation's materialistic way of life. If lay and ordained church people in the Protestant and Roman Catholic churches continue to see budgets, promotional literature, manipulative techniques, shallow homilies on "giving," and, in some quarters, thinly veiled coercive measures as "stewardship," God, weary of a church that ignores *his* stewardship, may use other means and other people in other places to save his world from destruction. God's love is immeasurably wide; it is also structured by his righteousness. The fear of the Lord is not the end of wisdom, but it is the *beginning* of wisdom.

God seeks a new awakening, a new inbreathing of his Spirit in the lives of his people. For that to happen, the church must leave the lonely heights of spiritual omnipotence and meet its Lord in the valleys of human need.

Ordained and lay leaders who take biblical stewardship seriously will challenge church members to reexamine the priorities of their own lives, the church, and society in the light of God's revelation and encourage them to readjust their life-styles to reflect the demands of the gospel. When that happens, fundamental changes will be called for on all fronts, both personal and communal. But the narrow, parochial, institutional fund-raising approach to stewardship that has been used in most congregations is not sufficient to make this challenge. The American church will either learn to address itself more responsibly to the realities of human need and the implications of biblical stewardship or it may become an anachronism in American society within another generation. Of course, God's work will go on through other people and other agencies in other places. Presently, the American church is under his judgment.

Pain and travail are inevitable by-products of a serious, sustained effort to understand and do biblical stewardship. The congregation that addresses itself responsibly to the demands of the gospel will be brought into conflict with a society that seeks only to serve itself at the expense of natural and human resources, a society that disdains human life with body counts and triage ethics, and that sacrifices honesty and justice on the altars of national security.

Struggle and conflict will also result in the congregation itself, because church members are the same people who make the choices in the mainstream of American society. Few are prepared to pay the price of biblical stewardship—to take up their cross and follow Christ into the corridors of power, the ghettoes of the poor, and the homes of the spiritually impoverished affluent. Most church members fail to find the strength offered through the resources of the gospel to do biblical stewardship, because they do not seek it or are unwilling to pay the cost of it. Yet, some *are* persuaded to be servants of the Word, to serve God rather than mammon, to live lives that are more Christ-oriented than self-indulgent.

There are resources in the gospel that offset the high cost of Christian discipleship. The blood of the crucified God has paid the price for us. But we are not above our Master. We must pay a price too. "Biblical stewardship is a life-style with the Cross at its center. The church must challenge, inform, and persuade its own community to embody God's Word in the world if it expects to be a force in society rather than a fungus on it." [23]

For Discussion

1. Are there biblical grounds for developing a personal gospel or a social gospel, each distinct from the other? Has this division happened in many congregations during the last quarter of a century? Has it happened in our congregation? Discuss.

2. Is it possible to preach the whole counsel of God (his Word in the Old and New Testaments), yet focus the church's ministry *only* on the individual needs of our parishioners? Read Amos. Study Jesus' parables. Discuss.

3. Can a congregation forge a ministry from the resources of the Word that focuses on social concerns while neglecting the care of church members? Discuss.

4. A biblical ministry is not prophetic, *or* pastoral, personal *or* social; it is instead prophetic *and* pastoral, personal *and* social. Agree? Disagree? Discuss, using biblical and theological documentation.

5. Chapter 5 sets forth specific questions on how the church and state relate in the United States. Consider some or all of them. There is no neat answer to any of the questions posed, and presently, there are no full-bodied answers to most of them. Does the gospel expect us to address these and other moral questions in society as ably and honestly as we can in our congregation? Is this what stewardship involves? Discuss. Identify and discuss other moral social questions that are not posed in Chapter 5.

CONCLUSION

W E HAVE EXAMINED SOME OF THE means the church has employed over the centuries to support and advance its institutional life and to do Christ's work in the world. The picture is ambiguous except for the first several centuries. It still is in most American congregations. We have also examined the nature of biblical stewardship and some of its theological and practical implications for people living in the community of faith in America today. These implications are mind-boggling. Acted on, they will be disturbing and disruptive, but also healing and empowering. They will be costly to persons and congregations. The theological and practical implications of biblical stewardship call for repentance and gospel faith in those (laity as well as clergy) who are appointed to administer the congregation's life and work and in the whole membership of the congregation as well.

God's grace covers the earth as the waters cover the sea. He offers power and hope in Christ for those who trust enough to do his commandments, to sing his song in an alien land. Will the church recover from its missed opportunities in this century to proclaim concretely and teach specifically the truth of God's stewardship? The mission is there. The strength is there. God's stewardship *can* be done in our fragmented, ghettoed, self-indulgent society. Tens of thousands of congregations across this country have the choice to make *now*. They can put on the armor of God's righteousness and serve Christ in the devastatingly difficult choices that the world sets before them or they can live out their lives seeking only their own survival while taking refuge in the bunkers of pride, piety, and sanctity. That, as Kierkegaard observed more than a century ago, is what makes human freedom "dreadful."

The question before each congregation is whether it will pay the cost of Christian discipleship. Some congregations that are struggling seriously to do so are alive, vibrant, and glowing in locations and situations that once appeared to be inhospitable to the gospel. But the basic test of any congregation's stewardship is not the size of its harvest but its *fidelity* to the Word of God. On that test, congregations, like individuals, live or die daily. God pleads: "Choose life . . ." (Deut. 30:15); and in Christ, each congregation can!

Notes

1. See Wallace E. Fisher, *From Tradition to Mission* (Nashville: Abingdon, 1965), Apex, 1974, for a first-hand account of establishing a *biblical* ministry in an old, urban, declining church (Trinity, Lancaster, Pennsylvania, 1730). Teaching biblical stewardship was and is a large strand in this ministry.

2. See Kenneth Scott Latourette, *A History of the Expansion of Christianity*, vol. 5, *The Great Century* (New York: Harper & Row, 1943).

3. See Wallace E. Fisher, *Stand Fast in Faith* (Nashville: Abingdon, 1978), Chapter 4.

4. Ibid., Chapter 6.

5. See Wallace E. Fisher, *A New Climate for Stewardship* (Nashville: Abingdon, 1976), Chapter 2 for a fuller discussion.

6. Ibid., Chapter 3.

7. Helge Brattgård, *God's Stewards* (Minneapolis: Augsburg, 1963), pp. 22-188. To my knowledge, this is the best study available on the biblical roots of stewardship.

107

8. See *Tradition to Mission*, Chapter 4, "Dialogue and Encounter," for a report from a congregation.

9. Ibid., Chapter 1, "Illusion and Reality."

10. Wallace E. Fisher, *Because We Have Good News* (Nashville: Abingdon, 1974). See especially Chapter 3, "The Integrity of the Evangelizing Congregation."

11. See *New Climate*, "Stewardship of the Self," pp. 58-73.

12. Ibid., pp. 68-69.

13. See especially Wallace E. Fisher, *Preface to Parish Renewal* (Nashville: Abingdon, 1968), Chapter 4, "The Significance of Leadership." Cf. also *Tradition to Mission*, p. 14.

14. The same criterion should be applied to invested funds administered by national church bodies.

15. See *Stand Fast*, "Introduction."

16. See Richard Klinger, *Simple Justice* (New York: Harper & Row, 1976).

17. *New Climate*, pp. 86-87.

18. See Wallace E. Fisher, *Politics, Poker, and Piety: A Cultural Perspective on Religion in America* (Nashville: Abingdon, 1972), Chapter 5, "The Church and the State in America."

19. Oscar Cullmann, *The State in the New Testament* (New York: Scribner's, 1956), p. 3.

20. See H. Richard Niebuhr, *Christ and Culture* (New York: Harper & Row, 1956).

21. See *Politics, Poker, and Piety*, Chapter 5.

22. Ibid., Chapters 3 and 4, "The American" and "Dissent in America."

23. *New Climate*, p. 15.

For Further Reading

Bauman, Pieter M. *Can the World Share the Wealth?* (New York: Friendship Press, 1969). An insightful, informative study.

Brattgård, Helge. *God's Stewards* (Minneapolis: Augsburg, 1963). The best treatment on biblical stewardship in print.

Brooks, Paul. *The House of Life* (Greenwich, Conn.: Fawcett, 1972), chapters 17-20. Informative, sobering.

Brown, L. David. *Take Care* (Minneapolis: Augsburg, 1978). Focuses on the Christian care of persons.

Cullmann, Oscar. *The State in the New Testament* (New York: Scribner's, 1956). An indispensable study.

Garrett, De Bell, ed., *The Environmental Handbook* (New York: Ballantine Books, 1970). An excellent survey; a solid introduction to ecology.

Elder, Frederick. *Crisis in Eden* (Nashville: Abingdon Press, 1970). Biblical basis for ecology.

The Fabulous Century, 1960-1970 (New York: Time-Life Books, 1973). Pictures and texts from the '60s.

Fisher, Wallace E. Book titles listed in Notes.

Fuchs, Victor. *Who Shall Live? Health, Economics and Social Change* (New York: Basic Books, 1975). A challenging call for adequate health care in the United States.

Galbraith, John. *The Affluent Society* (New York: Scribner's, 1959, revised). A seminal work in American social-economic-political history.

Gunn, Frank W. *Churches and Taxation* (Board of Social Ministry, Lutheran Church in America, 1971). Brief but informative.

Kantonen, T. A. *Theology of Stewardship* (Philadelphia: Fortress, 1956). In a narrow historical sense it is what it claims to be.

Katz, Harvey. *Give! Who Gets Your Charity Dollars?* (Anchor Books: Garden City, N.J., Doubleday, 1974). Journalistic, informative.

Kelley, Dean. *Should Churches Be Taxed?* (New York: Harper & Row, 1977). A solid study. Kelley takes the negative approach to the question and says so plainly.

Larsen, Martin A. and Lowell, C. Stanley. *Praise the Lord for Tax Exemption* (Washington and New York: Robert P. Luce, 1969). Journalistic, superficial, yet suggestive.

Mayer, Milton. *On Liberty: Man v. The State* (Santa Barbara: The Center for the Study of Democratic Institutions, 1969). An excellent study from the humanists' point of view.

Moule, C. F. D. *Man and Nature in the New Testament* (Philadelphia: Fortress, 1967). Insightful, sometimes brilliantly so.

Powell, Luther P. "Stewardship in the History of the Christian Church," in Thompson's *Stewardship in Contemporary Life,* appended below. An excellent survey.

Robertson, D. B. *Should Churches Be Taxed?* (Philadelphia: Westminster, 1973). A useful survey.

Salstrand, P. T. *History of Stewardship in the United States* (Grand Rapids: Baker, 1956). Best work in its field.

Slater, Philip. *The Pursuit of Loneliness* (Boston: Beacon, 1971). A gifted philosopher's view of contemporary American society. Properly disturbing.

Thompson, T. K., ed., *Stewardship in Contemporary Life* (New York: Association, 1965). Still a useful work.

White, Lynn, Jr. "The Historical Roots of Our Ecological Crisis" in *Science,* March, 1967. White, a Stanford University professor of history, links the present ecological crisis to the influence of Judeo-Christian culture. Thomas S. Derr, a Smith College professor of history, has provided a substantial critique of White's arguments. See *Worldview,* January, 1975, p. 43. Both articles are valuable reading for biblical stewards.